ECONOMIC DEVELOPMENT IN
THE GULF STATES

IRFAN SHAHID

ii

Contents

iv

vi

Preface

Economic Development in the Gulf States is an essential textbook for the graduates studying the economic condition of the Gulf States. This book is written considering the needs of undergraduate students pursuing any degree course in art, social science, management and banking.

The book provides a succinct summary of theories studied under the subject of economic development. It will help students to comprehend the core concept of economic development and economic growth. The book discusses the various features and characteristics of developed and underdeveloped economies.

Furthermore, the book provides an outline of gulf countries, including their productivities, governance and economic achievements. International Trade Organization plays a significant role in the flow of International Trade. The book provides the detail of various international organisations involved in international Trade. A brief discussion also made on the formation and establishment of OAPEC and OPEC.

The last chapter of the book covers the industrial development of the gulf economy. It discusses the various features and process of industrialisation in the Gulf States.

Hope this book will be equally useful for the students and general readers who want to understand the economic, political and social condition of the Gulf countries.

Irfan Shahid
Assistant Professor
Department of Economics and Business Studies
Mazoon College, Muscat

CHAPTER I
Economic Growth and Economic Development

Economic growth is referred to the increase of per capita real gross domestic product (GDP) over a period. Real GDP is the quantitative concept since it involves increased productive capacity in an economy, which leads to rising national incomes and living standards over time.

In contrast, Economic development is a qualitative process that refers to a structural change of economic and social infrastructure in an economy, which allows an increase in the standard of living in a nation's population. Economic growth and development can vary from different countries, depend on their level of income, quality of life, environmental quality and the government's involvement in the economy.

Difference between Economic Growth and Development

ECONOMIC GROWTH	ECONOMIC DEVELOPMENT
The term economic growth refers to an increase over time in a country's real output.	It implies progressive changes in the socio-economic structure of an economy.
Growth is a gradual and steady change, in the long run, this comes about by a gradual increase in the rate of saving and population.	Development is a discontinuous and spontaneous change in the stationary state.

Economic growth is related to a sustained quantitative increase in the country's per capita income.	Economic development is a broader term and is related to the qualitative change in economic wants, goods, incentives and institution.

Indicators of Economic Growth and Development

Economist usually measures economic growth in terms of **gross domestic product** (GDP) or related indicators such as **gross national product** (GNP) or **gross national income** (GNI) which is derived from GDP calculation. GDP is calculated from a country's national accounts which report annual data on incomes, expenditure and investment for each sector of the economy.

Gross Domestic Product (GDP) is the money value of all goods and services produced in the domestic territory of an economy for a period in a year.

GNP is derived by adjusting GDP to include repatriated income that was earned abroad and excludes expatriated income that was earned domestically by foreigners.

Gross National Product (GNP) is the money value of all final products and services produced by the nationals in a country.

In countries where inflows and outflows of this sort are significant, GNP may be a more appropriate indicator of a nation's income than GDP.

The formula for calculating GDP

$GDP = C + I + G + (X - M)$

Where as

C stand for Consumption level

I stand for Investment level

G stand for Government Expenditure

X stand for export

M stands for Import

GNP = GDP + Net income from abroad

GDP is the most commonly used method for economic development. It is annually used by every country to estimate their level of consumption, investment and government expenditure. It is used for further planning and development. Besides gross domestic product, there are some exclusive methods for the measurement of economic development such as the Human Development Index, Harrod Domar Model, but we will discuss only the Human Development Index.

Human Development Index

The weaknesses inherent in the use of GDP as a measure of development have led to the creation of other measures. The most well-known of these is the **Human Development Index (HDI)** which regularly publishes by **The United Nations Development Programme (UNDP)** in its *Human Development Report.* The HDI is a composite index that rates countries according to their overall performance about three criteria

- Life expectancy
- Education
- Per Capita GDP

The HDI was created by the Pakistani economist Mahbub Ul Haq and the Indian economist Amartya Sen in 1990. The HDI sets a minimum and a maximum for each dimension, called goalposts, and then shows where each country stands about these goalposts, and then shows where each country stands about these goalposts, expressed as a value in between 0 and 1.

The HDI of Oman is 0.821, which belongs to the group of countries having high HDI according to UNDP data.

Meaning of a Developed Country and a Developing Country

A **developed** country is one which has achieved maximum economic development where there is high per capita income; high standard of living and natural resources are almost fully utilised.

A **developing** country is one which is achieving progress in primary, secondary and tertiary sectors by using its resources.

Features of a Developing Economy

Developing countries are classified as low-income, middle-income, newly-industrialised, and oil exporting. The developing countries have several common features and problems.

1) General Poverty and Low standard of living
2) Burden of Internal and External Debt
3) Low Per Capita Income
4) Over Dependence on Agriculture
5) Backwards Industrial Sector
6) Unemployment
7) Low level of Productivity, The Productivity level is very low in underdeveloped countries as compared to developed countries. Low level of productivity is due to the economic backwardness of people, lack of skill, illiteracy and ill-training.
8) Dualistic Economy Dualistic Economy refers to the existence of advanced and modern sectors with traditional and backward sectors.
9) Inappropriate use of natural resources.
10) Limited foreign Trade.

The Main Constraints or Limits of Economic Growth

Lack of Proper Infrastructure

Infrastructure includes capital such as ports, transport, networks, energy, power and water supplies and telecommunication networks. Poor infrastructure hampers growth because it causes higher costs and delays for businesses, reduces the mobility of labour and hits the ability of export businesses to get their products to international markets.

Dependence on Limited Exports

Many nations still relying on specialising and then exporting low value added primary commodities and the prices of these goods could be highly volatile on world markets. When prices fall, an economy will see a sharp reduction in export incomes, a higher trade deficit.

Low National Savings and Low Absolute Savings

Savings needed to provide finance for investment. In many smaller low-income countries, high levels of poverty make it almost impossible to generate sufficient savings to provide the funds needed to fund investments projects. This increases reliance on international borrowing or tied aid.

Limited Access to Financial Capital

Limited access to financial capital and poorly developed domestic capital –this is particularly the case for many small, low-income countries.

Corruption and Poor Governance

Corruption and poor management always create mischief in economy. It never let grow development and innovation. It leads to the wastage and underutilisation of a country's resources.

Rising Inflation

Inflation refers to a persistent rise in the general price level for a certain period. It is observed that inflation reduces the purchasing power of an individual, discourages the consumption and reduces the production in an economy.

Persistent Trade Deficits due to Rising Imports

Some countries may experience large and widening deficits on the current account of their balance of payments. This means that the value of imported goods and services is greater than the value of exports and net investment incomes leading to an outflow of money from their economy. High trade deficits might have to be covered by foreign borrowing or reliance on inflows of capital investment from overseas multinationals. And large trade gaps can eventually lead to a currency crisis and possible loss of investor confidence.

Inadequate Investment in Human Capital

Sustained growth requires long term improvements in productivity, research and development and innovation. Inadequate investment in human capital may result in deficiency in the production of economy and reduce the level of consumption in an economy.

Weakness in Promoting and Supporting Entrepreneurship

It is one of the most common hurdles to economic growth. Underdeveloped economy lacking in supporting entrepreneurship and investment.

The Vicious Circle of Poverty

In economics, the circle of poverty is the "set of factors or events by which poverty once started is likely to continue unless there is an outside intervention".

Many developing countries are caught up in the vicious circle of poverty. Poverty is accompanied by low levels of education, literacy and skill; these, in turn, prevent the adaptation to new and improved technologies and lead to rapid population growth. Successful development may require taking steps to break up the chain at many points.

Overcoming the barriers of poverty often requires a concentrated effort on many fronts and a 'big push' is required to break this 'vicious circle' into a 'virtuous circle'. If the country has stepped to invest more, improve health and education, develop labour skills, and kerb population growth, she can break the vicious circle of poverty and stimulate a virtuous circle of rapid economic growth.

A country is poor and remains poor because its human and natural resources remain not utilised. In the less developed countries, people are mostly unskilled and technologically backwards. They are illiterate and lack entrepreneurial ability. So the natural resources are not used properly, output remains low and poor country remains poor because it is poor.

How to Break the Vicious Circle of Poverty?

Remaining poor is indeed no crime. The accepting of poverty and allowing it to continue is certainly a crime. Briefly, the vicious circle of poverty can be broken in developing countries by adopting the following measures.

1) Increase in savings
2) Higher per capita growth rate

3) Efficient use of natural resources
4) Employment of human resources
5) Increasing the stock of capital goods
6) Technological advance
7) Role of the government
8) Role of advanced nations. The advanced nations can help the less developed countries in breaking the poverty barrier by
   i)   Expanding the volume of Trade with them
   ii) increasing the flow of private and public basic infrastructure
   iii) Provision of direct aid in primary social sectors such as education, health, etc.
   iv) Provision of soft loans for development
   v)   Writing off loans

Theories of Economic Growth

The Classical Theory of Growth

A theory of economic growth that argues that economic growth will end because of an increasing population and limited resources. Classical Growth Theory economists believed that temporary increases in real GDP per person would cause a population explosion that would consequently decrease real GDP.

Neo-Classical Theory of Growth

An economic theory that outlines how a steady economic growth rate will be accomplished with the proper amounts of the three driving forces; labour, capital and technology. Neo-Classical economists believe that to raise an economy's long-term trend rate of growth requires an increase in the labour supply and an improvement in the productivity of labour and capital. When a new technology becomes available, the labour and capital need to be adjusted to maintain growth equilibrium.

The Rostow's Stages of Growth

It is one of the significant historical models of economic growth. W.W Rostow developed it. The model postulates that economic growth occurs in five basic stages, of varying length.

1) Traditional Society
2) Preconditions for takeoff
3) Take- off
4) Drive to maturity
5) Age of High Mass consumption

Traditional Society

- Characterised by subsistence agriculture or hunting and gathering; almost wholly a "primary" sector

- Limited technology
- A static or "rigid" society; lack of class or individual economic mobility, with stability prioritised and changes negatively.

Preconditions to Take off

- External demand for raw materials initiates economic change
- Development of more productive, commercial agriculture and cash crops not consumed by producers and largely exported
- Widespread and enhanced investment in changes to the physical environment to expand production (i.e. irrigation, canals, ports)
- Increasing the spread of technology and advances in existing technology
- Changing social structure, with previous social equilibrium now in flux
- Individual social mobility begins
- Development of national identity and shared economic interests.

Take off Stage

- Manufacturing begins to rationalise and scale increases in a few leading industries, as goods are made both for export and domestic consumption
- The "secondary" (goods-producing) sector expands and the ratio of secondary vs primary sectors in the economy shifts quickly towards the secondary stage
- Textiles and apparel are usually first to "take off" industry, as happened in Great Britain's classic "Industrial Revolution."

Drive to Maturity

- Diversification of the industrial base; multiple industries expand and new ones take root quickly
- Manufacturing shifts from investment driven (capital goods) towards consumer durables and domestic consumption
- The rapid development of transportation infrastructure
- Large-scale investment in social infrastructure (schools, universities, hospitals, etc.)

Age of Mass Consumption

- The industrial base dominates the economy; the primary sector is of greatly diminished weight in economy and society
- Widespread and normative consumption of high-value consumer goods (e.g. automobiles)
- Consumers typically (if not universally), have disposable income, beyond all basic needs, for additional goods.

Suggested Readings

Gillis, M., Perkins, D. H., Roemer, M., & Snodgrass, D. R. (1992). Economics of development (No. Ed. 3). WW Norton & Company, Inc.

Ray, D. (1998). Development economics. Princeton University Press.

Aghion, P., & Howitt, P. W. (2008). The economics of growth. MIT press.

Mellor, J. W. (1976). New economics of growth. Cornell University Press.

CHAPTER II
GULF COOPERATION COUNCIL
An Overview of GCC

The Gulf Co-operation Council (GCC) was formed in 1981 to create economic, scientific and business cooperation among oil exporting members. These Middle East countries share the common faith of Islam, an Arabian culture, an economic interest separate from OPEC. On a per capita basis, they are among the wealthiest countries in the world. The Gulf Co-operation Council headquarters is in Riyadh, the capital of Saudi Arabia, its largest member. Together, they supply one-third of the U.S. oil and own up to $225 billion of the U.S. debt. These countries are seeking to diversify their rapidly growing economies away from oil.

Arguably the most important article of GCC charter is Article 4, which states that the alliance was formed to strengthen relations among its member countries and to promote cooperation among the countries citizens. The GCC also has a defence planning council that coordinates military cooperation between member countries. The highest decision making entity of the GCC is the Supreme Council, which meets on an annual basis and consists of GCC heads of state. Decisions of the Supreme Council are adopted by unanimous approval. The Ministerial Council made up of foreign ministers or other government officials, meet every three months to implement the decisions of the Supreme Council and to propose a new policy. The administrative arm of the alliance is the office of the Secretariat General, which monitors policy implementation and arranges meetings. Some of the most important achievements of the GCC include the creation of Peninsula Shield Force, a joint military venture based in Saudi

Arabia, and the signing of an intelligence sharing pact in 2004. The GCC consists of six members

Profile of GCC Countries

The Kingdom of Bahrain

It is the largest island. The word "Bahrain" taken from an Arabic word "AL-Bahr". The literal meaning of Bahrain is two seas. Its 1.2 million people enjoy a GDP per capita of $40,500. Its economy grew by 4.5% in 2010. Oil was discovered in commercial quantities in Bahrain in June 1932. The first Gulf state to discover oil, it was also the first to reap the benefits that came with revenues, in a particular marked improvement in the quality of education and healthcare. By Gulf standards, Bahrain's oil reserves are quite small. To decrease its reliance on oil revenues, the government is striving to diversify Bahrain's economy by attracting more commercial companies, particularly in the IT field.

The Kingdom of Bahrain has 125 million barrels to proven crude oil reserves (0.03% of the GCC reserves and 0.01% of the world crude oil reserves). Bahrain possesses the lowest reserves among the GCC countries, which is presently producing 49,000 barrels of oil per day. Oil accounts for 11% of GDP (exclusive of allied industries), 60% of export earnings and 70% of government revenue.

Kuwait

Kuwait is one of the richest countries among GCC. The population of Kuwait is double than Bahrain. They enjoy the 10th highest standard of living ($48,900 per person). The country holds 9% o the world's oil reserves. Crude oil and refined products account for most of the country's exports. The reserves of crude oil are estimated to be 10% of the world total, the third largest quantity in the world. Kuwait's other main industries include desalination, food processing, and the manufacturing of building materials, which include plastics, cement, and metal pipes. Kuwait has a geographically small, rich, relatively open and oil-dominated economy with official proven crude oil reserves about 202 billion barrels- almost 7.4% of the world and 21.6% of the GCC crude oil reserves- the second largest among the GCC countries after Saudi Arabia.

Sultanate of Oman

It's a middle-income country with notable oil and gas resources and substantial Trade and budget surpluses. Petroleum accounts for 64% of total export earnings, 45% of government revenues and 50% of GDP. Hydrocarbon sector represents one of the most important sectors in the Omani economy. Oman possesses 5.50 billion barrels of proven crude oil reserves which account for 1.2% of the total GCC reserves- almost 0.% of the total world reserves.

The Kingdom of Saudi Arabia

The Kingdom of Saudi Arabia is the largest Arab country of the Middle East and GCC. It is bordered by Jordan and Iraq on the north and northeast, Kuwait, Qatar, Bahrain and the United Arab Emirates on the east, Oman on the southeast, and Yemen on the south.

Saudi Arabia is a founding member of the Gulf Cooperation Council (GCC).

With a population of around 32.6 million (2016) and nearly 20 per cent of the world's conventional oil reserves, Saudi Arabia is the Middle East's largest economy. Real GDP growth in 2015 was 3.4 per cent, according to the IMF. The recent decline in oil prices is expected to impact Saudi Arabia's current account balance in 2016 negatively.

Qatar

The economy of Qatar relies on oil and gas, which accounts for 50% of GDP, 85% of export earnings and 70% of government revenue. Oil and gas have made Qatar one of the world's fastest growing and higher per capita income countries in recent years. Sustained high oil prices and increased natural gas exports until late 2008 have helped build Qatar's budget and trade surpluses and foreign reserves. Presently, it has 15.21 billion barrels of proven crude oil reserves, representing 3.2% of the GCC oil reserves – almost 1.1% of the total world oil reserves. At its current level of production of about 776 thousand barrels per day, crude oil reserves will last for 54 years. Qatar is the richest among the GCC countries in terms of natural gas reserves, which stood at 25.26 trillion cubic meters at the end of 2008, representing 61% of the GCC total natural gas reserves and around 14% of the world reserves. Qatar can be seen as one of the most stable countries in the GCC region, given its combination of valuable natural resources and prudent macroeconomic management.

The United Arab Emirates

The United Arab Emirates (UAE) is situated in the Southeast of the Arabian Peninsula, bordering Oman and Saudi Arabia. In December 1971, the UAE became a federation of six emirates - Abu Dhabi, Dubai, Sharjah, Ajman, Umm Al-Quwain, and Fujairah, while the seventh emirate, Ras Al Khaimah, joined the federation in 1972. The capital city is Abu Dhabi, located in the largest and wealthiest of the seven emirates.

The UAE is the Middle East's second largest economy, after Saudi Arabia, and one of the wealthiest countries in the region on a per capita basis. Its current GDP in 2015 was estimated at US$339.1 billion, a real GDP growth rate of around 3.0 per cent. The UAE has six per cent of the world's oil reserves and the seventh largest proven natural gas reserves. Petroleum exports were US$126 billion in 2014.

MACROECONOMIC OVERVIEW
Growth

The year 2004 was the best in the history of the Saudi economy in terms of economic performance since 1982. After achieving robust growth in 2003 and 2004, Saudi Arabia is expected to achieve another prosperous year (2005), attributed to strength in the oil sector, best domestic geopolitical environment, acceleration of reform measures.

Bahrain is one of the most diversified economies in the GCC region. The government is making strenuous efforts to attract foreign investors and pursue limited privatisation to achieve the ultimate goal of economic diversification to reduce the country's dependence on oil. Aluminium is Bahrain's second major export after oil. Bahrain's economic activity is dominated by oil (processing), and the economy is developing downstream aluminium industries as well. Oman's public finances are heavily dependent on oil earnings, which account for around 67% of public revenues. The governmental fiscal policy has played a significant role in pursuing Omanization, diversification and privatisation.

The UAE is the second largest economy in the region, recording one of the highest economic growth rates in the Arab region because of its growing oil and gas exports and on-going economic diversification programs Saudi Arabia has been commended for its "extraordinary low inflation" in a survey of 12 Arab countries by the World Economic Forum (WEF) recently. The Kingdom has a proven track record of low inflation rates over a long period of time. Almost other GCC states also maintain a low inflation rate. The Fiscal policy of GCC states is very second due to higher oil revenues they are gaining with a hike in oil prices since last six years. The monetary policy of Saudi Arabia will remain focused on maintaining a fixed exchange rate regime with the US Dollar (US$). The kingdom has realised very high levels of trade surpluses on the back of bullish oil market trends. The first practical measure under the economic agreement was the elimination of custom duties between member states from March 1, 1983, on all agricultural, animal, industrial, and natural resource products of the national region.

The GCC Commercial Arbitration Centre was created in December 1993 to settle trade disputes between GCC citizens with each other, and between them and foreigners.

In October 2001, the Gulf States removed a major obstacle to speed up the creation of a custom union by agreeing on a mechanism to share duties on imports jointly.

The main benefits enjoyed by the GCC nationals with the formation of GCC

In order to encourage GCC citizens to expand their economic and professional activities throughout the GCC states, Article 8 of the UEA instructs the member states to give all GCC citizens the same treatment as granted to their own citizens without any discrimination or differentiation in the following fields.

1. Freedom of movement, work and residence
2. The right of ownership, inheritance and bequest
3. Freedom to exercise an economic activity
4. Free movement of capital.

Suggested Readings

Nakhleh, E. A. (1986). The Gulf Cooperation Council Policies, Problems and Prospects.

Ramazani, R. K., Ramazani, R. K., & Kechichian, J. A. (1988). The Gulf cooperation council Record and analysis. University of Virginia Press.

Kamrava, M. (Ed.). (2011). International politics of the Persian Gulf. Syracuse University Press.

Yousef Khalifa Al-Yousef (2017) The Gulf Cooperation Council States Hereditary Succession, Oil and Foreign Powers, Saqi Books

CHAPTER III
Economic Integration

Economic Integration

The term used to describe how different aspects of economies are integrated. As economic integration increases, the barrier of Trade between markets diminishes. The most integrated economy today, between independent nations, is the European Union and its Euro Zone.

The degree of economic integration can be categorised into five stages.

1. Preferential Trade Area
2. Free Trade Area
3. Customs Union
4. Common Market
5. Economic and Monetary Union

Preferential Trade Area

A trade pact between countries that reduces tariffs for certain products to the countries who sign the agreement. While the tariffs are not necessarily eliminated, they are lower than countries not part of the agreement. A Preferential Trade Area (also Preferential Trade Agreement, PTA) is a trading block which gives preferential access to certain products from the participating countries. A PTA can be established through a trade pact. It is the first stage of economic integration.

Free Trade Area

Free Trade is a type of trade bloc, a designated group of countries that have agreed to eliminate tariffs, quotas and preferences on most (if not all) goods and services traded between them. It can be considered as the second stage of economic integration.

Unlike Custom Union, members of a free trade area do not have a standard external tariff (same policies concerning non-members) meaning different quotas and customs. Free trade aims to reduce barriers for easy exchange, the business can grow as a result of specialisation, a division of labour, and most importantly via (the theory and practice of) comparative advantage.

A free trade area allows free Trade among members, but each member can have its own policy towards non-member countries. Example The North American Free Trade Area (NAFTA) creates a free trade area.

Custom Union

A custom union is a trade bloc which is composed of a free trade area with a common external tariff.

Common Market

A common market is a custom union with free factor movements (especially labour) among members. Example The European Union (EU) is a full customs union.

Trade Creation

Trade Creation is a process by which low-cost imports from other member countries replace high-cost domestic production.

Trade Diversion

Trade Diversion occurs with the replacement of low-cost imports from non-member countries with higher cost imports from member countries.

An example of trade diversion is the UK's Import of lamb. Before Britain joined the EU, most lamb imports came from New Zealand, the cheapest lamb producers. However, when Britain joined the EU, the common external tariff made it more expensive to import lamb from New Zealand than from countries inside the union.

Thus France became the majority exporter of lamb to the UK. Trade was diverse from New Zealand and created between France and the UK.

Trade Bloc

A trade bloc is a type of intergovernmental agreement, often part of a regional intergovernmental organisation, where regional barriers to trade (tariffs and non-tariff barriers) are reduced or eliminated among the participating states.

EU-GCC Free Trade Agreement

In 1991 the Council authorised the commission to negotiate a Free Trade Agreement with the countries of the Gulf Co-operation (GCC), i.e. Bahrain, Kuwait, Oman, Qatar, Saudi Arabia and the United Arab Emirates. The conclusion of such agreement was made conditional upon the establishment of a customs union among GCC member states.

In December 2001, the GCC Heads of States decided to advance the entry into force of a GCC customs union to January 2003 and to simplify the Common External Tariff to two groups products that are exempted of duties and products with 5% duty. This decision encouraged both parties to proceed more rapidly in the negotiations. The Common External Tariff is in effect since 1st January 2003 with some exceptions. The intention is for the agreement to cover all areas of trade relations; notably industrial, fisheries and agricultural goods.

Trade Picture

The Gulf Cooperation Council is currently the EU's fifth largest export market. Meanwhile, the EU is the first trading partner for the Gulf.

- EU exports to GCC are diverse but focused on machinery and transport materials (46.5%), for example, power generation plants, railway locomotives and aircraft as well as electrical machinery and mechanical appliances.
- EU imports from GCC are mainly fuels and derivatives.

Suggested Readings

Balassa, B. (2013). The theory of economic integration (Routledge revivals). Routledge.

Scitovsky, T. (2013). Economic Theory and Western European Integration. Routledge.

Gabel, M. J. (1998). Economic integration and mass politics Market liberalisation and public attitudes in the European Union. American Journal of Political Science, 936-953.

El-Agraa, A. M., Bulmer-Thomas, V., & Price, V. C. (1997). Economic integration worldwide. Basingstoke, Hants Macmillan.

CHAPTER IV
INTERNATIONAL ORGANISATIONS

General Agreement on Tariffs and Trade (GATT)

GATT was formed in 1947 and signed into international law on January 1, 1948. GATT remained one of the focal features of international trade agreements until it was replaced by the birth of the World Trade Organization on the 1st January 1995. The foundation for GATT was laid by the proposal of the international trade organisation in 1945. GATT's main objective was to reduce the barriers of international trade through the reduction of tariffs, quotas and subsidies.

Functions of GATT

1) The GATT has organised many trade negotiations. As a result of these negotiations, the tariff rates on thousands of items entered into world trade were reduced or bound against the increase. The developed countries achieved a 50% reduction in many industrial products.
2) The agreement also provides proper safeguards for the domestic industry and Trade.
3) It also solves trade disputes among members, countries impartially, amicably and quickly.

Objectives of the GATT

1) *Reducing the tariff barrier and promoting Free Trade*
2) *Developing full use of resources of the world*
3) *Expansion and promotion of International Trade*
4) *Ensuring Full Employment and a large and steadily growing volume of Real Income and Effective Demand*

5) *Providing equal opportunities to all countries in term of Trade in International Market*
6) *To provide amicable solutions to a dispute related to International Trade*

The World Trade Organization (WTO)

By the late 1980s, there were calls for a stronger multilateral organisation to monitor trade and resolve trade disputes. Following the completion of the Uruguay Round (1986-94) of multilateral trade negotiations, the WTO began operations on January 1, 1995. The Uruguay Round ended with the decision to dissolve GATT and establish the more powerful and more institutionalised World Trade Organization (WTO) in 1995.

The World Trade Organization (WTO) is the only international organisation dealing with the global rules of trade among nations. World Trade Organization (WTO), international organisation established to supervise and liberalise world trade. Its primary function is to ensure that trade flows smoothly, predictably and freely as possible.

The WTO is the successor to the General Agreement on Tariffs and Trade (GATT), which was created in 1947, replaced by a specialised agency of the United Nations (UN) to be called the International Trade Organization (ITO). Although the ITO never materialised, the GATT proved remarkably successful in liberalising world trade. It has its headquarters in Geneva, Switzerland and, by 2016, had 164 member counties, including Yemen, which was the last major nation to join. Roberto Azevedo is selected Director General again in the council meeting held on 28 February 2017 for the second term will start from the 1st September 2017

Objectives of WTO

1) *Administering WTO trade agreements*
2) *Providing a platform for trade negotiations*
3) *Handling trade disputes*
4) *Monitoring national trade policies of member countries*
5) *Technical assistance and training for developing countries*
6) *Cooperation with other international organisations*

How is the WTO different from GATT?

1-The GATT was a set of rules, a multilateral agreement, with no institutional foundation, only a small associated secretariat which had its origins in the attempt to establish an International Trade Organization in the 1940s. The WTO is a permanent institution with its own secretariat.

2-The GATT rules applied to trade in merchandise goods. In addition to goods, the WTO covers Trade in services and trade-related aspects of intellectual property.

3-GATT system allows existing domestic legislation to continue even if it violated the GATT agreement but WTO does not permit this.

4-GATT is less powerful and dispute settlement mechanism was less efficient while WTO is more powerful and dispute settlement is more efficient.

Principles / Characteristics of WTO Trading System

The World Trade Organization is based on the following core-principles or characteristics

1-Trade without Discrimination

The main principle in the charter of the World Trade Organization is to promote international Trade without any discrimination. This principle is further elaborated into two – MFN and national treatment (a) Most-favoured-nation (MFN)- treating other people equally (b) National treatment - Treating foreigners and locals equally.

The rules embodied in both the GATT and the WTO serves certain purposes. First, they attempt to protect the interests of small and weak countries against discriminatory trade practices of large and powerful countries. The WTO's Most-Favoured-Nation (MFN clause) and national-treatment rules stipulate that each WTO member must grant equal market access to all other members and that domestic and foreign supplier must be treated equally.

2-Free Trade

First of all, it should be noted here that the WTO is not for free Trade at any cost. It is all about lowering trade barriers between trading countries. The barriers concerned include customs duties (or tariffs) and measures such as import bans or quotas that restrict quantities selectively.

3-Predictability

With stability and predictability, investment is encouraged, jobs are created, and consumers can fully enjoy the benefits of competition – choice and lower prices.

There are other ways as well to improve predictability and stability. One way is to discourage the use of quotas and other measures used to set limits on quantities of imports. Another way is to make countries trade rules as clear and transport as possible.

4-Promoting fair competition

WTO is a system of rules dedicated to open, fair and undistorted competition. The rules on non-discrimination – MFN and national treatment – are designed to secure fair conditions of trade. So these rules also apply to the dumping and subsidies. Many of the other

WTO agreements aim to support fair competition, for example, in agriculture, intellectual property, services, etc.

5-Encouraging Development and Economic Reforms

The WTO system contributes to development. On the other hand, developing countries need flexibility in the time they take to implement the system's agreements. Over 3/4th of WTO members are developing countries and countries in transition to market economies.

Benefits of Joining the World Trade Organization

The main objective of this organisation to facilitate the movement of trade and commerce in member countries. WTO may help to non-member countries also, but complete help and official support one should get after joining the membership of WTO. A member can avail the following benefit from World Trade Organization.

1-The system helps to promote peace through following ways

a) Helping Trade to flow smoothly
b) Providing countries with a constructive and fair outlet for dealing with disputes over trade issues.

2-Disputes are handled constructively

The WTO system helps resolve these disputes peacefully and constructively.

3- A system makes Trade easier for members.

4-Free Trade cuts the costs of living.

5-It provides more choices of products and qualities.

6-Trade raises incomes.

Lowering trade barriers allows Trade to increase, which adds to incomes – national incomes and personal incomes.

7-Trade stimulates economic growth

Exchange of goods through Trade and commerce enhances the productivities and level of competition in the manufacturing sector. However, it induces growth and development in the economy.

8-The basic principles to make Trade more efficient

One of the essential features of WTO is that it provides efficiency in the international trade mechanism. Such principles include non-discriminatory Trade, transparency, increased certainty in trade conditions, simplification and standardisation of customs procedures, removal of red-tapism, removal of bureaucracy, centralised databases of information, and such other measures that come under the head 'trade facilitation'.

The WTO's trading system doesn't claim that everything is perfect. Otherwise, there would be no need for further negotiations and for the system to evolve and reform continually.

The organisation of the Petroleum Exporting Countries (OPEC)

OPEC is an International Organisation of eleven developing countries which are heavily reliant on oil revenues as their main source of income. Membership is open to any country which is a substantial net exporter of oil and which shares the ideals of the organisation. The current Members are Algeria, Indonesia, Iran, Iraq, Kuwait, Libya, Nigeria, Qatar, Saudi Arabia, the United Arab Emirates and Venezuela.

Since oil revenues are so vital for the economic development of these nations, they aim to bring stability and harmony to the oil market by adjusting their oil output to help ensure a balance between supply and demand. Twice a year, or more frequently if required, the Oil and Energy Ministers of the OPEC Members meet to decide on the organisation's output level, and consider whether any action to adjust output is necessary in the light of recent and anticipated oil market developments. OPEC's eleven Members collectively supply about 40 per cent of the world's oil output and possess more than three-quarters of the world's total proven crude oil reserves.

Formation of OPEC

OPEC was formed at a meeting held on September 14, 1960, in Baghdad, Iraq, by five Founder Members Iran, Kuwait, Saudi Arabia and Venezuela. OPEC was registered with the United Nations Secretariat on November 6, 1962.

Key Functions of OPEC

1-It coordinates the oil production policies

2-Help oil producers to achieve a reasonable rate

3-Try to stabilise the market

4-Maintaining stability in oil production

How Does OPEC Stabilise the Market Price of Oil?

The OPEC Statute requires OPEC to pursue stability and harmony in the petroleum market for the benefit of both oil producers and consumers. To this end, OPEC Member countries respond to market fundamentals and forecast development by co-coordinating their petroleum policies. Production limits are simply one possible response. If demand grows, or some oil producers are producing less oil, OPEC can increase its oil production in order to prevent a sudden rise in prices. OPEC might also reduce its oil production in response to a market condition in order to counter falling prices.

How does OPEC influence the World Economy?

OPEC is mostly involved in the oil market, but it has long been aware of the need for improvements in world trade.

Back in 1975, OPEC was part of the calls for the creation of a new international economic order based on justice, mutual understanding and a genuine concern for the wellbeing of all people of the world. OPEC also called on the industrialised and developing countries to get together in order to solve the problems of poor countries and to look for a way to establish a better economic system by allowing more Trade and more exchange of knowledge between developing and OECD countries.

The OPEC Member Countries establishing the OPEC Fund for International Development in 1976 in order to assist non-OPEC developing countries in improving their economies, including their Trade. The OPEC Fund has been active in many regions, including Asia, Africa, Latin America, the Middle East and the Caribbean. The OPEC Fund has supported a range of different types of projects, from providing clean water and energy to remote communities, to building houses, school, hospital and roads and developing industry, farming and trade opportunities.

OPEC also assists in other ways by supporting developing countries efforts to help themselves; by helping to remove trade barriers in individual countries and on an international level, for instance through the World Trade Organization; and by supporting the world to maintain a stable economic system, based on steady supplies of oil at a reasonable price.

Impact of OPEC Policies on the Global Economy

It is apparent that the impact of OPEC policies on the global economy depends on its ability to control prices and supply of oil. With regard to prices, the observation is that price increases hurt the global economy, whereas price cuts aggravate global economic activity. However, in the wake of diminishing OPEC influence in controlling the price of oil, it is evident that OPEC policies pose a minimal impact on the global economy, especially at a time when industrialised economies are looking for means to reduce over-dependence on OPEC and focusing on alternative forms of energy

Environmental policies of OPEC

1-OPEC support sound environmental policies that are fair and equitable, based on proven needs and designed to address those needs.

2-OPEC is concerned about the environment and wanted to ensure that it is clean and healthy for future generations.

3-OPEC also support sustainable economic development, which required steady supplies of energy at reasonable prices.

4-OPEC is also spending heavily to improve its environmental impact, by locating sources of higher quality oil and gas, by developing cleaner fuels for consumers, and by reducing the impact of its activities through safer, cleaner drilling, transportation and refining processes.

5-OPEC also participates in many international meetings in order to remind governments and others who are debating environmental policies that they must consider the needs of developing countries, especially those that rely on their income from oil.

The organisation of Arab Petroleum Exporting Countries (OAPEC)

OAPEC was established in 1968 by Kuwait, Libya and Saudi Arabia. Its other members include Algeria, Bahrain, Egypt, Iraq, Qatar, Syria, Tunisia and the United Arab Emirates. Although they have several members in common, OPEC is a separate and distinct entity from OPEC (the Organization of Petroleum Exporting Countries), the 12-nation cartel that plays a pivotal part in determining global petroleum prices. At present, the OAPEC includes 10 members Algeria, Bahrain, Egypt, Iraq, Qatar, Syria, Tunisia and the United Arab Emirates.

Aims of OAPEC

1-To carry out common projects that would achieve a diversified economic investment for the members. This, in turn, would lessen their dependency on petroleum as a sole source of income. And consequently, this would slow down the consumption of their petroleum and prolong the period of its investment for future generations.

2-To consider the legitimate rights of the consumer by making sure that petroleum reaches the market under just and reasonable conditions.

3-To develop and promote the international petroleum industry by means of providing suitable circumstances for capital and experience to be invested in member countries.

Objectives of OAPEC

1-To coordinate relations among Arab institutions concerned with energy and development.

2-To identify and assess existing Arab resources and the efforts exerted to develop energy sources as well as the coordination and development of such efforts.

3-To identify and evaluate the impact of international energy policies on the Arab countries.

4-To study present and future Arab energy requirements and the means of satisfying them.

Suggested Readings

Rittberger, V., Zangl, B., & Kruck, A. (2012). International organisation. Macmillan International Higher Education.

Weiss, T. G., & Wilkinson, R. (Eds, 2013). International organisation and global governance. Routledge.

Krugman, P., Helpman, E., & Razin, A. (1991). International Trade Policy.

Griffin, J. M., & Teece, D. J. (2016). OPEC behaviour and world oil prices. Routledge.

CHAPTER V
Industrialisation and Diversification in GCC

Industrialisation

The process of social and economic change that transforms a human group from an agrarian society into an industrial one. It is a part of a broader modernisation process, where social change and economic development are closely related with technological innovation.

Diversification

It refers to the shifting of resources from the primary production to the secondary or tertiary sector.

Diversification 'normally refers to exports and specifically to policies aiming to reduce the dependence on a limited number of export commodities that may be subject to price and volume fluctuations or secular declines'. That aims of diversification are spreading risk by creating a variety of income sources; Industrialisation in its broadest understanding is the process of creating these diverse income sources.

Two ways of Diversification

Horizontal Diversification

New opportunities are sought for new products within the same sector, e.g., for example, Coca Cola could expand horizontally by offering alternative soft drinks if you investigate you will find out that Coco-Cola also sells Oasis, vitamins water, Fanta etc. when Coco Cola was the partners of McDonald's, so you had noticed that McDonald's ONLY sell Coco-Cola Products.

Vertical Diversification

Adding more stages of processing of domestic or imported inputs as it encourages forward and backward linkage in the economy, as the output of one activity becomes the input of another, thus upgrading the value-added produced locally. Coco Cola buying farmland to produce sugar beet for the choke, then purchasing factories to make the bottles cups etc.

Backward Linkages

It can be defined as "the growth of an industry leads to the growth of the industries that supply inputs to it."

Forward Linkage

It exists when the growth of an industry leads to the increase of other industries that uses its output as input.

The main factors that led to economic diversification in GCC countries were

- Income from hydrocarbons is finite, fluctuates and is practically the only source of the wealth-have placed the issues of economic diversification on the political agenda in the Gulf countries since oil was discovered.
- To reduce the dependence on oil.
- To generate more employment opportunities for the growing population.

Types of Industrialisation

The manufacturing sectors fall into two categories Export-oriented industries and import-substitution industries.

Export-oriented Industrialisation (EOI)

Sometimes, it is called export substitution industrialisation (ESI), export-led industrialisation (ELI), or export-led growth is a trade and economic policy aiming to speed up the industrialisation process of a country by exporting goods for which the nation has a comparative advantage

Export-oriented Industries

It includes oil-based industries. In addition to the extraction of oil and gas, the oil-based industries include refineries, the vast petrochemical sector and energy-intensive industries such as aluminium. As pointed out, oil-based industries are usually large-scale and capital-intensive projects and as such, generally state owned.

Import-substitution Industrialisation

An economic strategy aimed at encouraging national industrial growth to reduce imports of manufactured goods.

Import substitution is meant to generate employment, reduce foreign exchange demand, stimulate innovation, and make the country self-reliant in critical areas such as food, defence, and advanced technology.

The import substitution Industries

It includes a diverse set of activities, most commonly food processing and the manufacture of construction materials. The latter includes the production of the cement, steel, aluminium window frames, building cladding etc. These industries are usually small, labour-intensive and often privately owned.

The need for private sector involvement in Economic Diversification

- Private sector involvement is very much necessary for the success of diversification. If they invest in and operate tourism facilities, manufacturing industries, harbours, etc., they can no doubt provide a push towards creating a non-oil economy, non-oil exports and non-oil revenue sources.

- Another reason for the call for increased private sector involvement is that it can generate more foreign direct investment. FDI brings not only capital, but it can generate more employment opportunities also for the economy.

- Another reason is that, under the current allocation state model, only a relatively small part of the local population is involved in economic activities, and they do not need to focus on creating a productive base.

Diversification entails a broad societal process, which transforms a country from a single source of income, in this case, oil or gas, to a society where multiple sources of income are generated across the primary, secondary and tertiary sectors, and where large sections of the population participate. GCC countries share a shared vision for economic development highlighting the need for economic diversification of productive base, diversification through the establishment of import-substitution industries is potentially much closer to the original aim of divesting away from oil.

The measures taken to achieve Economic Diversification in GCC countries are as follows.

1. **The development of the physical and social infrastructure**
   Investments in infrastructure, schooling and, not least, health services, as such investments were deemed necessary for non-oil economy growth;

2. **The development of capital-intensive industries**
   It utilises the region's comparative advantage in hydrocarbon resources, for example, production of steel, aluminium, fertiliser and petrochemicals (i.e. chemical components derived from oil which serve as building blocks for products such as detergents, adhesives, plastics, fibres, lubricants and gels)

3. **The development of other manufacturing industries**, for example, cement, construction materials (plaster, cladding,

rebar, window frames, etc.), electrical products, textiles, clothing, furniture and household items.

4. **The development of other productive sectors and services**, for example, agriculture (animal production, poultry, dairy products), trade, banking, financial services and, since the early 2000s, aviation, real estate, tourism and significant buy-up overseas firms (e.g. hotel chains, harbours, real estate) to be managed from the Gulf.

5. **The reduction of the direct role of the public sector** as an agent of economic growth by privatising publicly owned companies and utilities and reducing domestic subsidies.

EXAMPLE

Diversification in the agricultural sector develops newer and other additional sectors like dairy farming, arable farming, milk and dairy products, meat and meat products, fruit, vegetables and so on.

Major arguments for diversification for a single resource or a delectable resource economy have centred on

1. Avoiding shocks of adverse terms of trade between primary commodities and manufactured products.
2. Encouraging domestic resources-based industrialisation and creating new sources of income.
3. Developing new economic sectors and promoting employment.
4. Strengthening inter-linkages in the different sectors of the economy

Resource Endowment and Industrialization in GCC

As petroleum and natural gas form the greatest volume of GCC resource, their industrial development has been directed mainly towards oil and gas-based industries such as petroleum refining, chemical fertilisers and petrochemical industries and/or to energy-intensive industries such as aluminium and steel. This goes in line with the concept of comp of comparative advantage, i.e. if countries specialise in producing commodities on the basis of their comparative advantage, returns from production and Trade will be maximised.

The availability of cheap energy resources is a blessing for GCC industrialisation. For example, the gas used as a feedstock to the petrochemical industry is associated with gas, and most of it is a by-product of crude oil production. The cost of producing this gas is meagre and if it is not used, it would have to be flared.

Developments in the level and efficiency of industrial capabilities of the GCC region enhanced the availability of some foreign investment attracting factors such as the skills available to prospective investors, the efficiency of local suppliers and service firms, and a network of supporting institutions, both private and public.

Challenges in the Diversification Strategy of GCC countries

The GCC countries lack diversification in the sustainable economic base and need to devise a system which encourages private investment in industry, agriculture, exports and re-exports, i.e., production and movement of goods the virtual absence of continuous local water resources and reliance on desalinated water, which is both expensive and insecure, is a constant challenge. Local food and agricultural production fall far short of providing self-reliance and security in light of a burgeoning population and evolving patterns of consumption. Population increase and a dramatic upsurge in education require finding appropriate employment for those with improved skills, as the present rate of growth in the non-oil sector leaves a widening gap between manpower supply and demand.

Suggested Readings

Jean-Francois Seznec (Editor), Mimi Kirk (Editor) (2012) Industrialisation in the Gulf A Socioeconomic Revolution (Routledge Studies in Middle Eastern Economics)

Hvidt, M. (2013). Economic diversification in GCC countries Past record and future trends.

El Beblawi, H. (2010). 11 Gulf industrialisation in perspective. Industrialisation in the Gulf A socio-economic revolution, 185.

Cook, F. D., & Nielson, K. (2010). 12 Industrializing Gulf society. Industrialisation in the Gulf A Socioeconomic Revolution, 198.

CHAPTER VI
Sustainable Development

Sustainability is the process suggested to improve the quality of human life within the limits of the global environment. It involves the solution for enhancing human welfare that does not result in degrading the environment on the wellbeing of other people.

Sustainable development has been defined in many ways, but most frequently quoted definition is from Our Common Future, also known as the Brundtland Report.

Sustainable development is an economic development that meets the needs of the present generation without compromising the ability of future generations to meet their own needs.

Living within our environmental limits is one of the central principles of sustainable development. But the focus of sustainable development is far broader than just the environment. It is also about ensuring a strong, healthy and just society. This means meeting the diverse needs of all people in existing and future communities, promoting personal wellbeing, social cohesion and inclusion, and creating equal opportunity.

Types of Resources

    a. Natural resources
    b. Human resources
    c. Human-made resources
    d. Entrepreneurial resources

Renewable Energy

"Renewable Energy-Resources that are naturally replenishing but flow-limited. They are virtually inexhaustible in duration but limited in the amount of energy that is available per unit of time".

Renewable sources of energy include wood, waste, geothermal, wind solar thermal energy", hydropower, ocean energy (thermal gradient, wave power and tidal power), biomass, draught animal power, fuelwood peat, oil shale and tar sands.

Non-renewable Energy

Non-renewable energy refers to energy sources that have limited availability. It is derived from materials that can be exhausted and cannot be recreated in a reasonable period of time. Sources of non-renewable energy include fossil fuels such as and coal, wood, and any substance that can be burned but not restored.

Renewable energy sources (RES) have significant potential to contribute the economic, social and environmental energy sustainability. They improve access to energy for most of the population, they also reduce emissions of local and global pollutants, and they may create local socio-economic development opportunities.

Renewable Energy Sources Advantages and Disadvantages

1. Solar

   Advantages infinite energy resource.

   Disadvantages of expensive manufacturing and implementing of solar panels.

2. Wind

   Advantages infinite energy resource.

   Disadvantages of expensive manufacturing and implementing of windmills and wind farms.

3. Tidal

   Advantages An enormous amount of energy could be generated in this way.

A barrage could be used in various ways as a bridge or as a barrage against flooding.

Disadvantages of the construction of barrage could be expensive. Wildlife could be affected.

4. Geothermal

Advantages infinite energy resource.

Disadvantages could be used just in volcanic regions.

Setting up could be expensive.

5. Biomass

Advantages infinite energy resource, if replaced.

Disadvantages of pollution with greenhouse gasses, when it's burnt.

6. Wood

Advantages of an available cheap source of energy.

Disadvantages of pollution with greenhouse gasses, when it's burnt.

If the process of replanting of trees is interrupted, it could become a non-renewable energy source.

Advantages of Non-Renewable Energy

One advantage of non-renewable energies is that right now, and they seem widely available and affordable. Oil and diesel are still good choices for powering vehicles. They are cost effective and much easier to produce and use. Non-renewable energy also has market value where the supplier or manufacturer makes money and pays workers enhancing economies.

Disadvantages of None-Renewable Energy

On the other side, there are many disadvantages to non-renewable energy. Because non-renewable energies come from sources on our planet, once they are gone, they can't be replaced or revitalised.

Pollution grows greater through the by-products they leave behind, and mining of non-renewable energy is causing damage to our environment. There is no doubt that fossil fuels contribute to global warming and to break humans of their habit to lean on non-renewable energy sources remains a challenge.

Aims and Objectives of Sustainable Development

1. Sustainable development aims to balance our economic, environmental and social needs, allowing prosperity for the present and future generations.

2. Sustainable development consists of a long-term, integrated approach to develop and achieve a healthy community by jointly addressing economic, environmental, and social issues while avoiding the overconsumption of key natural resources.

3. Sustainable development encourages us to conserve and enhance our resource base by gradually changing the way in which we develop and use technologies.

Countries must be allowed to meet their basic needs of employment, food, energy, water and sanitation. If this to be done sustainably, then there is a definite need for a sustainable level of population. Economic growth should be supported and developing nations should be allowed the growth of equal quality to developed countries.

Major problems faced by the developing countries in the path of their development, in context to GCC countries

The same challenges are increasingly confronting the Gulf Cooperation Council (GCC) countries that western countries have faced in terms of how to balance the need to develop their economies while at the same time taking into account the impact of such developments on the environment and on communities and individual; the classical concept of "profit" vs." planet" vs." people "or balancing the Triple Bottom Line of "environmental", "economic " and "social" sustainability. As the GCC countries develop their built environments- including commercial and non-commercial properties and their infrastructure; their industrial capacities –often through large-scale industrialisation programs; and their agricultural capacities, there are sustainability issues to consider. The Triple Bottom Line elements to be considered are environmental sustainability issues such as waste, recycling, water usage, energy- including the use of renewable, and pollutions; economic sustainability issues including employment opportunities for local people, education and training and engagement of business and individuals that make up the supply chains and finally, social sustainability issues such as safety at work, working hours, equality and sponsored by the Kuwait Foundation for the advancement of sciences(KFAS) 2 diversity, noise dust and pollution, traffic congestion, stakeholder engagement and community involvement in decision-making.

Rapid economic growth in the Gulf countries has led to also rapidly increasing energy consumption; this may be said to be the result of three distinct phenomena the first is the "normal" increase in energy consumption-especially electricity –for rapidly increasing and wealthier urban populations; the second is relative specialisation in an energy-intensive industry, notably petroleum refining, petrochemicals, cement, iron and steel, aluminium and other metal smelting and the like; the third is the pattern of very low efficiency in energy use caused by low prices discouraging investment in better homes, appliances etc. The Gulf countries are increasingly aware of environmental issues and specifically of climate change concerns and policies related to carbon emissions.

- Climate Change The world is on course of long-term global temperature increasing of 3.5C, according to the International Energy Agency (IEA). Some models predict that the GCC will experience temperature increases of up to 4 C by 2100 over much of the region. This is likely to lead to more frequent extreme events such as storms and cyclones and potential sea level rises which could flood land, threaten desalination plants and increase the salinity of freshwater resources, face massive species Extinctions, widespread starvation, declining production of crops, rising temperatures means increasing water demand and with falling freshwater levels and the increasing salinity in seawater.

- Energy & Fuel consumption Global fossil fuel markets are set to become more volatile and unpredictable due to growing worldwide energy demand, changes in consumption patterns, certainties around supply and production, and increasing regulatory interventions related to climate change. The Gulf countries face a difficult situation as they depend mainly on fossil fuels-the main cause of carbon dioxide (CO_2) emissions – and their economies are dependent on the oil, gas, and petrochemical industries. Though the rate of development is high, lack of arable land and water resources prevents the development of carbon sinks, forests, and green areas.

- Population Growth The GCC has one of the fastest-growing population in the world and by 2020is forecast to increase by one-third, to 53 million people, population growth will place intense pressures on the ecosystem and the supply of natural resources such as food, water, energy and materials. Unemployment is also one of the major challenges facing the GCC region, which has a fast-growing young population. Rapid population growth will remain concentrated in cities. This will put pressure on public services, infrastructure and housing in urban centres.

- Water Scarcity GCCs face severe water scarcity. Water-intensive industries such as agriculture, oil and gas and chemicals are especially exposed to water scarcity and price volatility. GCC countries are suffering from a huge deficit in their water resources reaching more than 20 billion meters, being met mainly by an intensive over drafting of renewable and non-renewable groundwater resources for the agricultural sector, and by the extensive installation of highly expensive desalination plants for the municipal sector, and by reusing a small percentage of treated wastewater in the agricultural and municipal sector. An opportunity exists for businesses in the region to reduce the water intensity of industrial processes, increase water re-use and recycling, and minimise waste.

- Food Security, more than 60 per cent of food in the GCC, is currently imported and GCC states are investing in agricultural production in Asia, Eastern Europe and Africa to ensure a continuous supply. Some 80 per cent of GCC freshwater resources are used in agriculture

- Urbanization Speedy urbanisation has been the dominant trend in the GCC over the past decade. As a result of this, energy demands are increasing day by day, putting pressure on the environment by increasing pollution etc.

The Need for Sustainable Development in GCC

Environmental protection and economic growth must go hand in hand. Population growth, water scarcity, climate change and other force are combining to present an increasingly complex challenge for economic growth and development. Development programs across the globe now recognise that faced with such an uncertain future, and traditional short-term thinking cannot provide a firm foundation for continuing development in economy .a long-term perspectives needed. They not only face particular risks due to the region's unique economic, geographic and political situations but must also adapt to capitalise on emerging development opportunities.

In the early 2000s, several countries in the GCC took strategic decisions to diversify their economies, transforming them from focus on a single commodity- oil- to range of profitable sectors. Construction and growth were priorities. Fast economic development has brought a rapid expansion of private wealth. But things are changing. Domestic energy and desalinated water demands have soared in recent years due to rapid population growth, high rates of urbanisation, increased economic activity and then harsh climate. Consumption of material resources and food has increased to unsustainable levels, putting pressure on supply chains and further threatening the region's food security. This fast-paced growth has brought fundamental change to the region's development approach and introduced new directions from policymakers.

Steps Taken to Achieve Sustainable Development

Aware of all these challenges, the GCC stated are undertaking a variety of measures to ensure long terms sustainability growth in various fields. The GCC countries have recently adopted a more pro-active approach to addressing environmental issues on all levels of international regional and national levels; such as;

1. Introducing energy-efficiency measures
2. Investing in clean fuel and renewable energy supplies
3. Improving water efficiency
4. Investing new water desalination capacity
5. Buying or leasing agricultural land abroad

Growing awareness is needed to address climates and sustainability issues. All companies operating in the region will need to become more energy and water efficient, and products will have to comply with energy efficiency standards.

Growing local energy demand is putting pressure on the GCC's hydrocarbon resources. As a result, the government in the region have started looking at alternative energy sources, such as solar, wind and nuclear, as a means to maintain economic development while reducing emissions.

Leadership in Energy and Environmental Design (LEED) standard will come into force in 2014, to increase energy efficiency and water conservative in all new buildings.

It was first introduced in Dubai by H.H. Sheikh Mohammed bin Rashid Al Maktoum (1147 building in the GCC region are currently either LEED registered) (The most well-known project based on energy efficiency and water conservation is the flagship Masdar initiative of Abu Dhabi.)LEED Registered projects in Oman Oman Botanical Garden, Oman Exhibition and Convention Centre, the Oberoi Resort at Al Khiran.

Also, several governments in the region are considering nuclear energy as a key substitute for oil or gas-fired power plants to meet growing electricity demand. Nuclear energy is capital intensive and an excellent store of value for the future it is the kind of investment that country with substantial financial resources and limited investment opportunities would logically find very attractive as a basis for long-run economic diversification and sustainability.

Water desalination requirements are the most obvious aspects of vulnerability and potential non-sustainability of the Gulf economies. Finding a reliable and sustainable solution for water desalination is, therefore, an essential aspect of GCC security and sustainability. The long-term survival of GCC countries requires sustainable sources of energy.

The achievement of sustainable development requires, primarily, the diversification of the production base of the economy. This is in order to reduce reliance on oil and increase the dependence on the other production activities. The National Income will thus diversify from a single source to many other renewable sources.

Why Should We Conserve Energy?

Energy needs to be conserved to protect our environment from drastic changes, to save the depleting resources for our future generations. The rate at which the energy is being produced and consumed can damage our world in many ways. In other words, it helps us to save the environment. We can reduce those impacts by consuming less energy. The cost of energy is rising every year. We need to realise how energy is useful to us and how can we avoid it getting wasted.

To starts saving energy is not a big thing at all. We can start saving the energy from our home itself, just by turning off the lights during day hours, washing clothes in cold water or using public transport instead of using our own vehicle and later can implement these things on much more extensive scale at a society level, then at city level then district level and finally at country level .you might notice a small change in your monthly bills by implementing these changes as they would be getting decreased more and more. With so many alternatives and so many techniques about there, if millions of people like us start doing these things, it will help us to save much more money and also help the environment.

Suggested Readings

Al-Maamary, H. M., Kazem, H. A., & Chaichan, M. T. (2017). Renewable energy and GCC States energy challenges in the 21st century A review. International Journal of Computation and Applied Sciences IJOCAAS, 2(1), 11-18.

David Bryde (Editor), Yusra Mouzughi (Editor), Turki Faisal Al Rasheed (Editor) (2015) Sustainable Development Challenges in the Arab States of the Gulf (The Gulf Research Center Book Series at Gerlach Press)

Elie Azar and Mohamed Abdel Raouf (2017) Sustainability in the Gulf Challenges and Opportunities (Routledge Explorations in Environmental Studies) Routledge